ISIDO

Young Martyr of the Congo

by
Jean Olwen Maynard

To Godfrey and Maureen Heyman

*All booklets are published thanks to the
generous support of the members of the
Catholic Truth Society*

CATHOLIC TRUTH SOCIETY
PUBLISHERS TO THE HOLY SEE

2

CONTENTS

Acknowledgments

The author expresses her thanks to the following sources: Enquiry of Fr Aloysius Dewitte and other documents used in the process of beatification, accessed through the Aequatoria Archive, University of Antwerp; and the Archives of the Sacred Heart Missionaries, Borgerhout; *"Isidore Bakanja Martyr? Mémoire de maîtrise"*, André Claessens (unpublished - Institut Catholique de Paris - 1978-79); *"Les Conflits dans l'equateur entre les Trappistes et la Société Anonyme Belge (1908-1914)"*, André Claessens (in Revue Africaine de Théologie, 4, 1980, nr 7, p 5-18); *"Bakanja Isidore, Martyr du Zaïre"*, Daniel Van Groenwegh (Didier Hatier - Brussels, 1989); *"Le Bienhereux Isidore Bakanja: La voix qui crie dans la forêt"*, Mgr Ignace Matondo Kwa Nzambi (Éditions L'Épiphanie - Limete-Kinshasa, 1994); *L'Osservatore Romano* (English Edition) 27 April 1994; *"Profiles in Holiness, Vol I"*, Redemptus Maria Valabek O Carm (Edizioni Carmelitane - Rome, 1996); *The Life of George Grenfell, Congo Missionary and Explorer"*, George Hawker (Fleming H Revell Co - New York, 1909); *"Political Awakening in the Congo"*, René Lemarchand (University of California Press, 1964); *"King Leopold's Ghost"*, Adam Hochschild (Macmillan - London, 1999); With very grateful thanks for the kind assistance of Michael Meeuwis of the University of Antwerp, and of Frs Honoré Vinck and André Claessens MSC.

INTRODUCTION

Who was Bakanja?

We hardly know anything about him. We don't even have a photograph to show us what he looked like. Born in a backwater, he never went to school. He lived under an exploitative colonial regime which automatically relegated him to underclass status in the country of his birth: a pair of hands and a strong back to produce wealth and services for the benefit of foreigners. The pinnacle of his short working career was landing a job as a domestic servant.

In a reflection on Bakanja's life written in 1994, addressed to the young people of today - and particularly to the young men and women of the Congo, whose long tragedy had still not ended - Mgr Matondo, Bishop of Molegbe shows how representative it is of the lives of so many millions of nameless others: all the world's people who "don't count".

At the threshold of adulthood Bakanja was brutally flogged by his employer's boss, for refusing to obey an unjust order, and died of his injuries.

Can such a life have meaning? Can it have anything to say to us? Can God bring something beautiful out of such a life? Isidore Bakanja's short life provides a most eloquent answer.

EXPLOITING THE CONGO COLONY

African Explorers

"The chief of the strangers was covered with cloth, and his face was white, and it shone like sun-light on the river..." Brief, vivid glimpses of Henry Morton Stanley floating down the Congo river with his Anglo-American Expedition passed into the folk memory of the people who lived along its banks. After crossing the entire continent of Africa from east to west, Stanley triumphantly emerged at the town of Boma, on the north side of the estuary where the great river flows into the Atlantic, in August 1877. He had driven his men mercilessly hard: his three white companions died en route, together with a large proportion of the African members of the expedition. Stanley returned alone to a hero's welcome in Europe.

As he made his way across France, he was approached by a well-dressed and obvious wealthy American, who introduced himself as General Henry Shelton Sanford. Sanford easily charmed the former workhouse lad. On behalf of Leopold II, King of the Belgians, he was empowered to offer Stanley a job, at a fabulous salary, with an international philanthropic association of which Leopold was chairman. To be headhunted by royalty must have been deeply flattering to Stanley. Even though for the moment he turned the proposal down, he didn't forget it.

Sanford received his refusal with gracious courtesy, and kept in touch. Later that same year, once it was clear that his native Britain had no immediate practical interest in colonial adventures in Central Africa, the famous explorer was ready to swallow Leopold's bait.

Colonising the Congo

Leopold was meanwhile working hard in his own way, pulling at diplomatic strings in Europe. His objective was to bring the western powers round to the idea of recognising the whole Congo basin as a colony, not of any one European country, but of his own international association. Leopold, the world was given to understand, was motivated by a disinterested concern to abolish the slave trade, promote scientific progress and commercial development, and bring the blessings of peace, civilisation and the Christian faith to the African people.

Trading links had long existed between the peoples of the African interior and the outside world. Traditionally, the most valuable commodity items had been human beings. Slavery was now illegal in Europe, and the slaving gangs which still operated in the interior could only market their captives to Arab countries. But demand for certain natural resources of the Congo basin - particularly

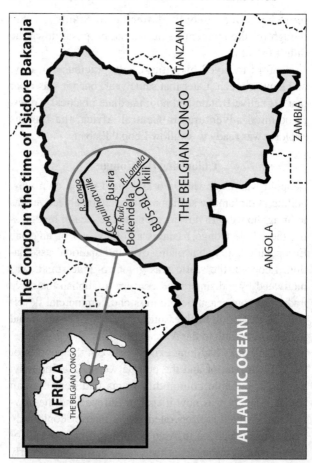

ivory and rubber - was growing keener. Trading companies, impatient with their dependence on African middle-
men, were eager to get closer to the sources of these valuable raw materials.

Until a few decades previously, it had been almost
impossible for Europeans to venture into the African interior and survive. The most daunting barrier was disease.
But a few key advances in medical practice - in particular
the systematic use of quinine as a prophylactic against
malaria - were now opening up the "dark continent".

In order to lay claim to the vast territory which, in his
own mind, he had already staked out, Leopold would need
to establish effective occupation in the shortest time possible, before anyone else beat him to it. He must line up
people ready to move in on his behalf, and form strategic
alliances with a variety of interest groups with reasons of
their own for wanting to penetrate into Africa. Key actors,
besides explorers and traders, would be missionaries.

Leopold was ready to extend the warmest possible
welcome to Protestant missionaries from Britain or the
USA, confident that they in their turn would help sway
public opinion in their home countries in his favour. The
first missionary expedition to take advantage, in 1878, of
the opening up of the Congo basin was led by the English
Baptist George Grenfell. Grenfell was later to render
invaluable service to Leopold by his voyages of explo-
ration into the interior.

Two years later a Catholic mission was established in Boma, by the Holy Ghost Fathers. Unfortunately, from Leopold's viewpoint, they were French - as were an over-whelming majority of all Catholic missionaries at that epoch. Leopold particularly did not want too many Frenchmen in his prospective colony: their presence could provide an excuse for France to move in on his patch. Yet Belgium was a predominantly Catholic country, and one in which the Church wielded considerable political clout. It was essential for his credibility to acquire Catholic missionaries for the Congo. He therefore began urgently canvassing Belgian religious congregations, and international ones that were at least not wholly French and might be in a position to deploy Belgian nationals. Refusing to give up in the face of their initial reluctance, he continued his urgings, offering generous financial subsidies to cover their travel expenses and settling-in costs.

King Leopold's hat trick

Though not personally present at the Berlin Conference in November 1884, he managed - by careful public relations work, and cleverly playing off one country against another - to achieve precisely what he wanted. On 29th May 1885 the birth of the "Congo Free State" was at last proclaimed, with Boma as its capital, and Leopold as its "King-Sovereign".

Sanford's lobbying skills had been invaluable to Leopold in securing recognition by the United States. The king found a cheap way of rewarding him by encouraging him to set up a commercial venture - misleadingly named the "Sanford Exploring Expedition" - to share in the exploitation of the natural resources of the Congo. Unfortunately Sanford, as Leopold well knew, had not a scrap of practical sense; his military rank was purely honourary and his vast wealth inherited. Like all his other business initiatives, the "Expedition" failed to thrive. After his death in 1890 it was taken over by the *Société Anonyme Belge* (SAB), a subsidiary of the company contracted to build a railway from Boma to Stanley Pool. The SAB quickly established an ivory market in Antwerp, then moved into rubber.

Running the Congo Free State

Within a few years the Congo Free State was represented on the ground by a few hundred white officials, military officers and commercial agents, thinly spread, effectively controlling a vast territory of around a million square miles and twenty million inhabitants. What made this possible was the overwhelming superiority, only recently developed, in military technology between the industrialised west and the rest of the world. As Hilaire Belloc put it:

Whatever happens, we have got
The Maxim Gun, and they have not.

The whites also supplemented their meagre numbers by deploying African allies and mercenaries. Some were brought from elsewhere on the continent but, because the population of the Congo comprised so many different ethnic groups, it was easy to apply a policy of divide and rule: chiefs would willingly support "Bulamatari" in punitive actions against rival tribes, and Congolese could usually be relied on to garrison territory inhabited by a different ethnic group from their own. In 1888 the African auxiliary troops were formally constituted as the "Force Publique". Commercial companies meanwhile organised their own private armies of black security guards, euphemistically termed "sentries".

To meet its manpower needs the state could have engaged free workers at a negotiated wage, as did missionaries and the earliest private traders, but in practice - and often as a matter of policy - relied largely on forced labour. Chiefs based in the vicinity of state enterprises were coerced into supplying "volunteers" - men who often had to be marched to their worksites chained together to prevent desertions en route. Relations between the state and the slave traders were quite ambivalent, since the state authorities which were supposed to be suppressing the slavers and rescuing the slaves were not powerful enough to take on the biggest gangs, and were quite prepared to purchase slaves from them to meet their own labour requirements. Captives who *were* rescued were not set free, but given the choice between contracting their services to the state as navvies or porters, or enlistment in the Force Publique. Discipline among the workforce, whether free or unfree, was enforced by the chicotte - a vicious rawhide whip.

Missionaries sent to Congo

In the 1890s ivory, initially the most valuable Congo product, was rapidly overtaken by rubber which was needed as a vital component for motor cars, bicycles and a variety of other new inventions. Huge plantations in Latin America and Asia were already being planted with *Hevea braziliensis*, the cultivable form of rubber tree. However it would take time for them to reach sufficient maturity to supply the rapidly growing demand. Meanwhile, rubber vines were to be found growing wild all over the Congo. At first, harvesting the rubber was relatively easy. But before long all vines within close reach of villages were exhausted - often cut down completely and grubbed up by the roots in order to extract the last drop of rubber - and increasing levels of coercion were needed to drive the collectors deeper and deeper into the jungle to find more.

From 1892 large tracts of the Congo were parcelled out as "concessions" to a small group of specially created companies, in which the state held 50% of the shares, while at the same time a vast expanse of territory was set aside as "Crown Domain", The companies were to enjoy an absolute commercial monopoly within their "concessions", while the state had similar rights within the Crown

Domain. The exclusion of free market competition narrowed down still further the Africans' options, and made it even easier to exploit their land and labour. The SAB, excluded from the the new concessionary system, naturally raised a furious protest. Backtracking slightly, Leopold agreed to allow 1,200,000 hectares within the Crown Domain to remain open to "free trade": in reality, the SAB was granted an effective monopoly over rubber gathering there. Lying between the Salonga and Lomela Rivers south of the town of Busira, which was the main SAB station, the enclave was referred to as the "Busira Bloc" - always, in practice, shortened to "Bus-Bloc".

By now several more Catholic missions had established themselves in the Congo. The Scheut Fathers arrived in 1887, followed six years later by the Jesuits. The Trappists of Westmalle Abbey had been approached by Leopold as early as 1876, but proved a harder nut to crack. Strict contemplatives, it made no sense at all to them to consider an active apostolate in Africa. After several refusals, Leopold put diplomatic pressure on the Vatican until at last, in 1893, Pope Leo XIII sent a direct order to the Abbot of Westmalle to comply with the king's wishes.

In 1894 the first party of five Trappists arrived in Boma to begin the gruelling three-week trek up Stanley's road. Within a few months they had identified a suitable location at Bamania, 10 km up the River Ruki from the important colonial settlement of Coquilhatville, which stood at the confluence with the Congo. A second party was already on its way from Westmalle. Meanwhile, there was no difficulty in hiring workers. Local men were so keen for jobs at the monastery that the missionaries found it extremely puzzling that, by contrast, they showed not the slightest interest in the Christian faith. It would be some time before they realised that the great attraction of mission employment was that it provided exemption from rubber collection.

To the east of Bamania, several days' journey by steamer, lay Bus-Bloc. But for the moment the wider local geography hardly concerned the newcomers. Their vision of what their evangelistic role should be was at first quite clear. They would build a monastery, strictly enclosed, and continue to devote their lives to contemplative prayer.

Care of displaced children

A rather different role earmarked for them by the colonial authorities was the care of "orphans". Child slaves, and other children who became separated from their families in the course of military actions, were euphemistically labelled "orphans" and placed in special state-run institutions - from which the boys automatically graduated into the Force Publique. Large numbers of children were constantly having to be placed, and all the missions were under pressure to take charge of some. The first contingent of boys was delivered to Bamania in 1896. When girls began to arrive an African woman, "Auntie Kee", was hired to look after them until some Dutch Sisters could be recruited from Europe.

The orphans at least provided a captive audience for religious instruction. A catechism had been obtained from the Scheut Fathers in the Kongo language, which was used around Stanley Pool. Like so many early missionaries, the Trappists took it for granted that any African language would do, and confidently made this text the basis for all catechetics and vernacular prayers.

The original Trappist vision for the future had had to be modified, but only slightly. The children would be brought up as Catholics, married off to each other, and settled on part of the monastery land as a Christian village. As an extension of the monastic complex, the village would be carefully preserved from all unnecessary contact with the outside "pagan" world. This was the official plan, but some of the Trappists actually in Africa were already beginning to have other ideas.

During the first half of 1899 numbers of mission staff fell very low, as some monks and Sisters died, and others had to be repatriated. But as soon as reinforcements came out, a sub-station was opened at Mpaku 50 km up the Ruki, with a view to outreach among the Pygmies. In succeeding years the area around Bamania was badly hit by epidemics of smallpox and sleeping sickness, during which the missionaries worked devotedly to care for the sick. Barriers crumbled as they came into real human contact with Africans, while for their part the Africans began to realise that these whites were different.

From 1901, outlying "farm-chapels" were founded from which priests or catechists, working alone or in pairs, could engage in evangelistic outreach to the non-Christian population. It wasn't easy to get the Trappists to realise that the Africans among whom they had settled - the Mongo peoples dwelling within the huge curve described by the upper reaches of the River Congo - couldn't understand their kiKongo catechism. But eventually the Vicar Apostolic, Mgr Camille Van Ronsle, intervened to insist that they learn the Mongo language. One Brother and one Sister were sent to take lessons at the Protestant mission in Bolenge, and in 1903 the first Catholic catechism was produced in loMongo.

Heart of Darkness

Wherever a state or company station was established in a suitable location for rubber collection, the surrounding villages were assigned quotas of dried sap to be delivered at regular intervals. To ensure that the quotas were not evaded, freedom of movement was severely restricted: in many places, Africans needed a written pass just to visit a friend in the next village. Agents usually tried to work through traditional authority structures, passing the burden of enforcement on to the local chiefs. Most chiefs were prepared to collaborate. They recognised they had no chance of defeating the whites militarily, and agents could sugar the pill by supporting "their" chiefs against political rivals, and hostile neighbouring tribes. Failure to deliver quotas - whether of "volunteers" or of rubber - was usually due not to recalcitrance but to the extreme difficulty of meeting the agents' insatiable demands. In such cases their reaction was swift and brutal.

A routine practice was to make captives of the village women, and hold them hostage until the quota was filled. Less routinely, but with distressing frequency, villages were burned down and their banana groves deliberately destroyed. The most ruthless agents simply killed a certain number of inhabitants "to encourage the others". Most of the actual killing was carried out by Force Publique soldiers and company "sentries". To prove they had killed the required number of people, and not wasted their ammunition, they were supposed to cut off the hands of their victims, preserve them by smoking, and present them in baskets for inspection back at the station.

Although Bus-Bloc was to acquire a sinister reputation, not much is known about what went on there in the early years. This is partly because the SAB archives have been lost, but possibly also because - compared with other areas, such as the huge "concession" allotted to the Anglo-Belgian

India Rubber Company - the level of abuse there was usually not so blatant. Abuse there certainly was. In the SAB's own personnel registers, comments were marked against all too many names: "brutal"; "heavy drinker"; "suspended"; "never re-employ" and, ominously, "dismissed for murder"! In 1901 K Jesperen, a Danish officer serving in the Force Publique, toured the countryside around Ngombe in Bus-Bloc, where SAB security guards had recently made an expedition in search of plunder. Jesperen was at first surprised by the hostility of the local people, but quickly discovered the reason when he saw the devastation in the villages. He reported finding, at places where the "sentries" had camped, large numbers of human bones which he believed were the remains of cannibal feasts.

Scandal and profit

By the turn of the century the Congo was showing a fat profit. Astronomical gains went to Leopold, who lavished them partly on improvements to his palaces, and partly on prestigious public building schemes to beautify the cities of Brussels and Ostend. Agents in Africa could expect to earn substantial commissions, and the concessionary companies were paying attractive dividends to their shareholders - the SAB being among the most successful. Everything seemed to be going well.

It was at this point that the scandal began to be blown wide open, as the result of a brilliant human rights campaign conducted from an office in Liverpool by Edmund Dene Morel. The British Consul in the Congo, an Irishman named Roger Casement, was ordered to proceed into the interior to conduct investigations into the rubber trade. His damning report, somewhat watered down by the Foreign Office for fear of diplomatic repercussions, was published early in 1904. Casement then teamed up with Morel to launch the Congo Reform Association.

Europe reeled in horror when Morel began publishing photographs showing the severed hands of victims, together with names, place and date. Leopold expressed concern and set up a Commission of Enquiry. Its worst findings were locked up in a top-secret archive in Brussels, but even the sanitised generalities which had to be made public brought the King-Sovereign under pressure to turn the Congo over to Belgium.

BAKANJA'S SHORT LIFE

Bakanja's early years

Away from the main centres of colonial activity and the worst trouble spots, life in the Congo could continue very much as before. Bakanja was born at the family home of his mother Inyuka, in a fishing community on the banks of the River Botato some distance west of Bus-Bloc. However his father, Yonzwa, was from the neighbouring farming settlement of Bokendela: a line of houses extending for several kilometres along the path which wound its way inland from the Botato. Together with his older brother Bokungu, and sister Nsombola, Bakanja grew up in Bokendela in an extended family household headed by his grandfather - parents, children and grandchildren, servants and clients, all living in a group of tiny grass huts clustered near together.

As soon as he was old enough, Bakanja began helping the men of his family in their work. One of their most important responsibilities was to clear new land for farming. Bakanja probably didn't have much to do with this: it was only needed from time to time, and the labour required was far too heavy for a small boy. But there were other tasks at which he could make himself very useful: collecting wild honey, nuts and fruits, and edible grubs. He also helped with the growing and cutting of raffia.

Working in the family

Routine cultivation of food crops wasn't men's work; in that sense the farmers of Africa were, and are, overwhelmingly the women. Inyuka hoed and weeded her garden, planted and dug up the cassava roots. She also had to gather firewood and prepare the cassava - a lengthy task involving several days of soaking, since the roots were poisonous if not properly treated before consumption. Being Yonzwa's sole wife had its advantages, but also meant there was no one to share the work - no one, at least, until little Nsombola grew old enough to help. It was hard work, certainly, but it would have been harder still to keep a family fed without it. The cassava plant, and the knowledge of how to cultivate and cook it, had made its way gradually to Bokendela perhaps two centuries before, passed from village to village all the way from the west coast where Portuguese traders had brought it from America. But Inyuka didn't know that. She was quite sure that women in Bokendela had been growing cassava since the world began.

Inyuka was also responsible for the banana grove, but that gave her very little trouble: banana trees could usually look after themselves. She taught Nsombola where to collect clay, how to fashion pots and bowls, and then how to build an oven from earth and palm branches in which to bake them till they were hard. Finally, it was Inyuka's job to manufacture salt for the family. It was obtained from certain plant products, including banana skins, and certain parts of certain types of palm-tree; a woman had to know exactly which. The salt was extracted by a long process of burning, filtering, soaking, boiling.

Bakanja was equally at home among his mother's as among his father's kin, and often collaborated in their fishing work. He learned to make fish-traps from raffia and forest fibres, and helped to set them in the shallows. He joined in the hunting of large fish and young crocodiles with fish-spears. Each year during the dry season, when the water-level sank and the fish began to migrate into the deeper parts of the river-system, he helped his maternal kin to collect palm branches and lianas, and weave them into large barriers to be erected across the Botato to force the fish into certain channels - where the nets were waiting. During this high fishing season, when the catch was particularly plentiful, work could continue well into the night, and most people didn't go home but camped out near the fishing grounds.

The fish could be eaten fresh, but a lot was smoked. Smoking, which was the work of the women, made it possible to preserve food for times when the catch was poor, or for trading with non-fishing communities. Each village had its market-day, when farmers exchanged agricultural produce for fish. Also on sale would be hoes and axes made from locally smelted iron, copper bracelets, ceramic pots, raffia cloth, palm beer and salt. These items could also be traded to the Pygmies in return for meat. The Pygmy hunter-gatherer bands which roamed the forest were well integrated into mutually co-operative relations with the majority Bantu population - so much so that the local Pygmies all now spoke loMongo, and had completely forgotten their own ancestral language. A number of Pygmies had settled in Bokendela as clients of farming families, and intermarriage was common.

Brave new world

In 1904, when Bakanja was about 16, he decided it was time to set out and see the world, learn new things, and start saving up money to buy himself a wife. Already his cousin Boya, son of his mother's sister Wela, had gone off upriver to find work with the SAB in Busira. Several other men from Bakanja's village were now making their own plans, and he was keen to go with them. After careful deliberation with the elders of their families, and mulling over the various scraps of information fed in to the village by returning workers, they decided to head downriver.

It was a great day for Bakanja when he finally took his place with his friends in a trading canoe about to set off down the Botato. The Botato flowed into a wider river which in turn led into the Ruki. Day after day went by, but at last the canoe reached the mouth of the Ruki. Even the Ruki was already so wide that from one bank it was impossible to see across to the other, and now Bakanja found himself staring open-mouthed at the vast expanse of the Congo.

Coquilhatville was expanding rapidly and new buildings were going up everywhere. Bakanja was taken on as a stonemason by a state-owned construction firm, working as assistant to the headman, Linganga. Linganga was very pleased with his new assistant, who was hard-working and easy to get on with. Bakanja for his part developed a great respect for the headman and - in common with a number of his workmates - was intrigued to discover that he was a Christian.

Bakanja meets Christianity

As yet there were very few Christians in Coquilhatville and, only a year or so previously, Linganga had been one of the first to be admitted to baptism. The first seeds were sown during the closing years of the nineteenth century when Corporal Raphael Itoto, a former "orphan" educated at a mission school in Boma, was posted to the the town's native garrison. Like so many "orphans", Itoto had found in the mission community a new family - the only family he could still look to - and his identification with the Catholic faith was solid. Each Saturday evening he set off up the path through the marshland alongside the Ruki to the Trappist mission at Bamania, to attend Sunday Mass the next morning. It was a three-hour trek each way. Nevertheless by 1900 he was bringing an eager crowd of friends along with him each weekend. The astonished missionaries counted over a hundred men, and about sixty women, all of whom Itoto was instructing as best he could.

In 1902 a farm-chapel was established at Boloko Wa Nsimba, only an hour's walk from the town, with two African catechists in charge. Fr Grégoire Van Dun arrived a year later, and it became a regular Mass centre with, before long, over 2,000 catechumens on its roll. Besides the soldiers and state employees from Coquilhatville, candidates were coming in from the surrounding villages, and from the workers on the state coffee plantations along the river. Bakanja began receiving instruction soon after his arrival. His catechist was Boniface Bankutu, a man of "simple, solid faith". According to Linganga, Bakanja was "very sweet and gentle in his character. Never any quarrels. He was a very good Christian." Bankutu acted as his sponsor when he was baptised, on 6th May 1906. By this time adult baptisms at the farm-chapel were quite common - on average about thirty took place each Sunday.

Baptism and "Habit of Mary"

From the moment of his baptism Bakanja adopted two clear marks of his new Christian identity. One was his "Christian name". In those days the custom of bestowing a recognised saint's name at baptism was enforced with the rigidity of a law, and Bankutu chose for his godson the name "Isidore". Immediately after the ceremony, the neophyte was also presented with a scapular.

Tradition traces the custom of wearing the scapular back to St Simon Stock, an English Carmelite who was elected General of the Order at a Chapter held in Aylesford in 1247. The story goes that Mary, Mother of God, appeared to Simon and promised him that whoever wore the scapular of Our Lady of Carmel would be saved. As used by laypeople, the scapular is a small piece of cloth worn on a string round the neck.

The Trappist missionaries in the Congo encouraged all their converts to wear the scapular, and take it very seriously: "When I see someone with the uniform of a soldier," they explained, "I immediately think that man is a soldier. When I see someone dressed as a policeman, I think that that is a policeman. Why do I think this way? Because I recognise them by means of their clothing. But how do you know if someone is a Christian? If he has a scapular of Mary and a rosary round his neck. That's how. This man is a Christian, he should show his faith to others." Taking this message very much to heart, the Africans always referred to the scapular as "Bonkoto wa Maria" - "habit of Mary".

Before Vatican II, in mission areas, Confirmation and First Communion were often delayed and followed only after additional courses of instruction. Bakanja was confirmed on 25th November 1906, and only on 8th August 1907 did he receive Our Lord for the first time in the Holy Eucharist. Soon after this Bakanja's contract came to an end, and he returned to his village. It was probably then that he built his own hut, near those of his immediate family. He was already planning for the future - a future in which he would marry, and have children of his own. As yet, however, there were no other Christians in Bokendela.

Difficulty in his new faith

Whereas Africans working in the colonial economy, far from their homes and families, usually treated Christian teachings with respect even if they were not ready to make any personal commitment to them, traditional communities did not. Going back to the village, Bakanja felt as though he had walked into a different mental universe, one which was at odds with his new-found faith. He had the sense of being uncomfortably stretched between two incompatible worlds, and there was nobody that he could turn to for moral support. Well, he was still young. For the moment, rather than settle down straightaway, he would go off once again to find work with Bulamatari, acquire fresh skills and save more money, and be part of a Christian community.

   This time, instead of returning to Coquilhatville, he made his way upriver to Busira and went to stay with his cousin Boya, who was working for the SAB there as a carpenter. There were already some African Christians in and around the town, and Boya was perhaps already one of them. Bakanja soon found employment as houseboy to an SAB agent named Reynders. In some ways domestic service was more difficult to get his head round than his previous job, since the white man's lifestyle was bewilderingly strange. Nevertheless the work itself was far easier than cutting stone, and the Belgian seemed remarkably reasonable and even-tempered. Bakanja felt he'd fallen on his feet this time.

"The whites don't like Christians"

In March 1908 the protracted negotiations between Leopold and the Belgian government over the transfer of the Congo were brought to a successful close. It was in June that year that Fr Grégoire Kaptein, the Bamania Superior, made a first exploratory visit to Busira. The Trappists were as yet still hampered in their outreach work by not having any boats of their own, so having to cadge lifts in state or private steamers, and this was the first time they had had anything to do directly with Bus-Bloc or the SAB. Fr Kaptein received an enthusiastic welcome from the black Catholics, who happily provided meals and accommodation for him. Normally, however, any white traveller would have been offered hospitality by one of the company agents. That this had not happened was both humiliating and worrying for Kaptein. It wasn't long before the catechists whom he stationed in Busira were reporting on attempts by senior SAB personnel to drive them out of the town.

Colonial policy as formulated in Belgium was, in principle, pro-missionary. True, Grenfell, along with most other Protestant missionaries, had ended up in the doghouse for supporting Edmund Morel's campaign. However under an agreement with the Vatican signed in 1906, all "national missions" - those maintained by organisations based in Belgium - were to enjoy continued favour, and substantial financial subsidies, from the colonial authorities. It was taken for granted that *Belgian* missions, out of patriotic loyalty, would refrain from troubling the government with embarrassing revelations, and since virtually all of them were Catholic, the Catholic hierarchy considered the agreement a great coup.

What happened out in the Congo, however, didn't always reflect official policy. Already the Trappists had come up against quite obstructive attitudes from the colonial civil service. A major cause must have been the strength of political Catholicism in the home country, which inevitably provoked a strong backlash within Belgian society - indeed, many Belgians were attracted out to the Congo by the dream of throwing off all constraints of religion and morality. Moreover the well-meaning insistence of some Catholic missionaries on relocating converts to mission property - whether for their own protection, or to enforce what they considered a properly Christian pattern of life - had been observed to create real problems. Idealistic officials deplored the disruption it caused to traditional communities, while the less idealistic resented missionary interference with their own plans for the African population.

Nevertheless, Fr Kaptein had never before come across anything like the virulent anti-clericalism he found in Bus-Bloc.

Towards the end of 1908, the SAB appointed Reynders as assistant manager on the Ikili rubber estate. Before taking up his new post he had to make a trip down the Salonga, during which his steamer made a stop at Bomputu. Bakanja took a stroll along the bank and got chatting to a houseboy named Boyoto, who was washing clothes in the river. Boyoto had previously worked at Bongila, an SAB estate further up the river, and when he learned where Bakanja was headed he warned him anxiously not to go with Reynders into Bus-Bloc. "The whites up there, they don't like people from downriver. And for you as a Christian it'll be even worse - the whites don't like Christians." However because Bakanja's relations with his employer had always been satisfactory, he refused to act on the warning.

Going to work at the Rubber Estate

On the way down the Lomela to Ikili a stop was made at
Bompende, where Reynders took on a second houseboy
named Bomandjoli. The SAB Plantation Inspector, a
German named Dörpinghaus, happened to be there at
the same time, and the two parties socialised. Because
the Africans couldn't make sense of European names or
remember them, they always made up their own names
for white people - names which had a meaning.
Dörpinghaus, Bakanja learned, was known as "Potama"
which means "Gash Cheek": the man had several
noticeable scars on his face - perhaps duelling scars of
the sort which it was fashionable for German students to
acquire at that period. Unusually among the SAB
agents, Dörpinghaus was a man of integrity, determined
to stick up for fairness and decency.

Ikili lay inland from the village of Iyele on the
Lomela. As the newcomers walked from the landing
stage through Iyele they noticed that all the huts were
newly built. Beyond the village the path led through
marshes followed by a strip of forestland. Emerging into
the sunlight again they found themselves entering the
plantation, with fields of young rubber saplings stretch-
ing away on either side. An old, disused traditional iron-
smelting furnace, made out of a termite nest, stood near
the path, which continued through rows of orange trees

and then forked. The right fork led to the African village
of Ikili from which the SAB estate took its name. The
left fork led to the sub-station of Isoko, further up the
Lomela. Reynders was to have particular responsibility
for Isoko, but he would not be expected to live there in
isolation; most of the time he could stay at Ikili where
he and the manager, Van Cauter, could enjoy each
other's company.

Bakanja and Bomandjoli were directed to the servants' quarters, a row of cabins standing in a line a short
distance to the rear of Van Cauter's big bungalow. There
they met Iyongo, Van Cauter's houseboy - a lad of about
12. They and Iyongo would be working quite closely
together. Mputu, the cook, lived in one cabin together
with his wife, and Bakanja was to share this with them.

Mputu offered to fix up a woman for him while he
was in Ikili, but Bakanja said no. Everyone thought this
very strange. There were plenty of women available, and
men who hadn't brought their permanent wives with
them were usually keen to set up temporary arrange-
ments, which were easily negotiated. Only, you had to be
careful to keep well away from those who served as con-
cubines to the whites. One of the cabins in the row was
set aside for them. Van Cauter currently had two,
brought with him from his previous posting at Bokaka,
and he was very jealous over them.

André van Cauter - Bakanja's persecutor

André Van Cauter had found in Africa his promised land, a vast untrammelled playground where he could do just about whatever he liked. His wife was safely in Belgium, and the law would never manage to catch up with him. After a first heady plunge into gun-running, illegal ivory trading and other shady activities, he'd settled down into his current niche in the SAB.

Cultivation of rubber in the Congo was only just beginning, and the trees on the Ikili plantations had still to reach maturity. The rubber which was crudely processed on the estate, inventoried, warehoused, and eventually loaded onto steamers for export was still collected from wild vines by the estate workers and the nearby African villages. The Belgian take-over had supposedly introduced reform, but rapid, radical change was impossible without making a clean sweep of personnel, which unfortunately was out of the question. Van Cauter, at any rate, continued to operate by the old methods. Shortly before Bakanja's arrival, he had burned Iyele down to punish the villagers for not fulfilling their quota.

On the plantation itself, the manager was notorious for his brutality and his sudden, inexplicable blinding rages. All the SAB agents, and virtually everyone in Bus-Bloc, knew his habits. Dörpinghaus couldn't stand him, and couldn't understand why the Commercial Director, Grillet, refused to make any attempt to moderate his behaviour.

Most of the officials and agents in the Congo were single, but a few were beginning to bring their wives out to join them, and Grillet was one of these. Planning a long, comfortable future for himself there, he had no intention of making waves. For the SAB, productivity and profit were all that mattered, and if he stuck his neck out and made trouble for his white colleagues there would be no future for him in Bus-Bloc. As for Van Cauter, Grillet had always got on quite well with him personally, and Van Cauter showed his appreciation for Grillet's understanding attitude by making frequent presents of ivory to Mme Grillet.

The usual name the Africans had for Van Cauter was *Longange*, and this was the one they used to his face. Behind his back they also referred to him as Esomb'a Nkoli, meaning "bundle of creepers". When he walked round the estate he usually carried in his hand a cat-o'-nine-tails made out of lianas cut from the jungle. Every so often he casually cracked it down on the back of any worker he thought was slacking. He was quite capable of hitting someone for nothing at all. For serious punishments he resorted to the chicotte. Recently a new whip made of elephant's hide, which he had laid out to dry on the verandah, had been found damaged - probably cut deliberately by one of the African workers. Instead of throwing it away, Van Cauter took a couple of nails from a packing case and used them to repair the whip. He cut down the points, but the nails still protruded slightly out of the leather. No one could tell whether he really intended to use it.

Christians disliked

The ways of the white men were often beyond comprehension, but something which had the estate workers more mystified than anything else was the way Van Cauter carried on about "Mon Père". Virtually all the SAB agents had a thing against missionaries, but Van Cauter's hatred of the Catholic Church was obsessional. "Mon Père" - "My Father", a respectful form of address used by a believer towards a priest - had become for him a mocking catch-phrase which he used constantly when ranting on about his fixation. He used it to refer not only to the clergy but to everything connected with Christianity, and he was completely undeterred by the fact that none of the Africans at Ikili could understand what he was talking about.

None of them had ever met a missionary or a catechist, or knew anything whatsoever about Christianity. When Bakanja arrived they were very interested to see him saying his prayers. Bomandjoli and some of the others asked to join him, and wanted him to teach them the words. But it wasn't long before Bakanja discovered that nothing sent Van Cauter into a worse rage than finding out that the workers were gathering together for prayer. He couldn't stand even the idea of Bakanja praying on his own, and forbade him to pray anywhere on the plantation.

"Pray in your heart"

So as not to provoke the man, Bakanja used to take himself off down the path that led towards Iyele. There was nothing unusual about that; any of the African employees might go down there during their off-duty hours, either for calls of nature or to wash out their clothes in a pool in the marsh. Surely it was no business of Van Cauter's if Bakanja also spent some time there saying his rosary - safely out of the white man's sight, and beyond the boundary of the rubber estate?

Once, without thinking, he took his rosary out of his pocket as he set off for the path. Van Cauter spotted it. "I don't want to see that thing here! Go and shut it up in your box. You're here to work, not mumble prayers!"

Reynders reacted to Van Cauter's harassment of his houseboy with cold indifference: "If you want to pray, pray in your heart. Don't do it so anyone can see you." Bakanja realised the warning he had been given was true: Reynders was a different person out here in the bush. Completely spineless, he would go along with whatever Van Cauter said - and he was learning to enjoy the sight of men cowering in fear in front of him.

Bakanja's fellow workers noticed that he was always very quiet and calm, and seemed very self-possessed. Towards the whites he was polite and somewhat reserved, but pleasant, and always a good worker. They couldn't understand why the manager had his knife into him.

Bakanja chose a time when Van Cauter and Reynders were both present to seek to resolve the impasse in which he found himself. "I came here to work for you, and you don't like me. I haven't stolen anything. I haven't neglected my duties. The best thing would be for you to give me a pass letter so I can go back in peace to my village."

Van Cauter snorted. "I'm not giving you a letter. You're in the God Squad - go and ask God for a letter!"

Flogged for wearing scapular

The SAB estate at Ikili drew most of its workforce from the immediate locality - particularly from the adjacent African village. Other Ikili villagers had found work at Bongila, another SAB estate which lay some 70 km off across country to the south-east. Among them was a woman named Loanga, who was living with one of the security guards. They weren't married, and after a while Loanga got fed up with the relationship and decided to go back home. She obtained a pass from the manager, Giret, and set off together with a fellow-villager employed on a neighbouring estate who was returning to Ikili at the same time. Half-way home, as they were passing near the village of Bonjoli, they were attacked and Loanga was killed. The man who was with her got away, reached Ikili safely and reported what had happened. The villagers went to complain to Van Cauter. Delighted at being handed an excuse for a bit of fun, he quickly got together a raiding party and, together with Reynders, set off for Bonjoli. The whites, security guards and estate huntsmen brought their guns, while the rest had bows and arrows. They arrived to find most of the men had already fled, apart from one who was shot dead as they moved in. The women were taken prisoner. Then, since the sun was going down, the raiders prepared to spend the night in Bonjoli.

The houseboys set up campbeds for the two white men and laid a table for supper. Suddenly Van Cauter caught sight of Bakanja's scapular and started yelling: "Take off that thing you've got round your neck!"

Bakanja went over to the fire where Mputu was busy with the cooking. "Longange has ordered me to take off my scapular. He says my 'habit of Mary' is disgusting, and he doesn't want to see any 'Mon Père' stuff round here." Iyongo and Bomandjoli were very surprised. Had Van Cauter really said that? "Yes," confirmed Bakanja.

Most of the Africans were afraid to nod off that night for fear that the locals would creep back and stab them where they lay, though the two whites appeared to sleep soundly. Next morning, on the way back to Ikili, they ran into an ambush. A son of the Ikili chief was killed by an arrow, but the Bonjoli men then ran off. Back at the estate their women were chained up inside a large shed whose official purpose was for smoking rubber, but which was also used unofficially as a prison.

Bakanja had discreetly moved his scapular well inside his shirt, but he had not removed it. A few days later, at breakfast, Van Cauter spotted the string sticking out and flew off the handle. "What's that supposed to mean? I ordered you to take that thing off."

"I'll not take it off," replied the houseboy. "If you want, take it off yourself but I'll not touch it!"

"I'll have you flogged!"

The manager was serious. He made Bakanja take off his shirt and lie down on the ground, and had him given 25 lashes. After the punishment was over, he put it around that Bakanja had spilled wine on the tablecloth at dinner the previous evening. The story had a superficial plausibility because how could anyone be sure it wasn't true? No one went into the common dining area, which the whites called their "mess", during mealtimes except the servants who were actually waiting at table. However staff who'd witnessed the flogging argued that at the time, Van Cauter had said nothing about spilled wine. He'd only been carrying on about "Mon Père".

Over a long, lazy drink that evening, Van Cauter put it to Reynders: "It won't bother you if I settle that one's hash for him?"

"No, do what you like. I don't need that 'boy' any more, so go ahead! It's true what you say; he's undermining white prestige, that Christian ..."

Visitors

The steamer "Brughman" called at the Iyele landing stage with Commercial Director Grillet, whom the Africans called Bongende, on board. A messenger was sent up to Ikili to explain that Bongende was on his way upriver to Isongu and didn't have time to stop, and to deliver a letter for Van Cauter warning him that an inspection was imminent.

Meanwhile the villagers of Bonjoli had gone off in their turn to Bongila, to complain to Giret, since it was to his estate that they were under obligation to deliver rubber. Giret knew he couldn't expect any more deliveries until the women were brought home. He put together a trekking party and set off for Ikili, planning to stay there for three days. That should give him plenty of time to talk to Van Cauter and get him to be reasonable. But before the end of the first morning he knew he'd made a wasted journey. Van Cauter was sticking to his demands that the villagers of Bonjoli ransom their women with copper bracelets. No ransom, no women. The bracelets would be paid to the Ikili village chief, as blood money for the deaths of two of his people: the woman Loanga and his son.

It was 2nd February 1909, the Feast of the Purification of the Blessed Virgin Mary. One of Giret's men, Boongo, was a Catholic. About midday, when it was time for Boongo to pray the Angelus, his companions asked him to wait a minute while they got everyone together.

Although they weren't Christians, they always liked to join in with Boongo when he said his prayers. As soon as the prayer started Iseboyo, the security guard, came up and told them to stop, as the Ikili manager didn't allow prayers. They ignored him until they'd finished the prayer, then turned on him. "What's that got to do with us? We aren't Longange's men. Who can stop us from praying?"

Bakanja had come up. He told Boongo: "The white man here has forbidden prayer. He doesn't want me to pray with other people - that's why I always pray alone. He doesn't even like me doing that. He told me, 'I forbid you to pray on the estate! I can't stand these 'Mon Père' people - they're not men, they're animals!'"

After serving lunch, Bakanja and Iyongo did the washing up and left everything tidy in the kitchen, then served coffee to the whites. Their duties finished for the time being, both strolled off across the stretch of open ground which lay between the mess and Van Cauter's large bungalow. There they separated, Iyongo making his way to the servants' quarters, while Bakanja turned onto the path that led to Iyele.

Van Cauter pursues Bakanja

The three whites remained seated at the table, sipping their coffee. Suddenly Van Cauter shouted to Iseboyo: "Take your gun and go kill Bakanja! I don't want any of those 'Mon Père' animals round here!"

Iseboyo went and searched the servants' quarters. The other domestic workers couldn't understand what was the matter: "How come you're going to kill Bakanja without knowing why?" Iseboya said he had no intention of killing him, only telling him that the white man was calling for him. Bakanja wasn't there, so he went back towards the mess. Meanwhile the manager had caught sight of Bakanja on the path, just disappearing among the orange trees. He told Iseboyo to go and look for him at the marsh, then went to the verandah of his bungalow to wait.

The houseboy hadn't even gone as far as the marsh before turning back towards the estate. Iseboyo met up with him by the old iron furnace, and brought him back to the bungalow. Looking up at Van Cauter Bakanja asked, "White man, why did you send for me?"

"Shut your jaw! retorted Van Cauter. "I've had enough of your tricks. If you go on like that all my men will believe your lies, they'll want to be baptised, and then no one will want to work any more. It's just lies you're teaching them - all these prayers and stuff you got from Mon Père!" He demanded to know where Bakanka was going along the path.

"I was going into the bushes."

"That's not true. You're lying!"

"I'm not lying!"

"You were going to Iyele. You wanted to tell tales on the boat! You were going to tell Bongende that I'm a bad white!"

"No. I wasn't going to the boat. I was going to the bushes."

Suddenly Van Cauter changed tack. "Lies! You weren't going to the toilet, you were going for that "Mon Père" stuff. Lie down!" He snapped to Iseboyo: "Flog him!"

"I can't," replied Iseboyo. "I've got a bad arm."

"Then go fetch Bongele!"

Bakanja fatally flogged

Reynders and Giret were watching from the verandah. Iyongo and Emeka, Giret's headman, stood behind. By now a number of other Africans were also on the scene, come to see what all the shouting was about. When Bongele, the Ikili headman, arrived Van Cauter handed him a whip and told him to flog Bakanja. Bongele asked what for.

"That's my business! I don't want any of these "Mon Père" people round here!" Turning to Bakanja, Van Cauter shouted, "Lie down!" Bakanja didn't move.

Stepping down from the verandah, he pointed to Bakanja's scapular. "What's that doing there? What did I tell you? Take it off your neck! Will you or won't you?" When Bakanja still made no move to obey, Van Cauter tore the scapular off and threw it on the ground. His dog caught it in his jaws and ran off to play with it, worrying it with his teeth. Meanwhile Van Cauter manhandled

Bakanja to the ground. He motioned to Iseboyo to take hold of his arms, and sent for the other guard, Bolonge, who was off-duty. Bolonge was made to hold Bakanja's legs. Van Cauter then ordered Bongele once again: "Flog him!"

"Not with this whip," protested Bongele. It's got nails in!"

"Don't give me that. It's no one's business except mine! Get on with it!"

Bongele took hold of the thin end of the whip, with the nails in, and began hitting Bakanja with the thicker handle-end. When Van Cauter saw what he was doing he yelled, "Not like that! Hit him with the nails!" Like everyone else on the estate, Bongele was terrified of Van Cauter. The overseer was now brandishing an axe handle he'd picked up. Bongele turned the whip round and continued hitting Bakanja, but as lightly as he could. Out of his mind with rage, Van Cauter screamed, "If you don't hit harder than that I'll kill the both of you!"

Bakanja had refused to take down his trousers for the beating, but the nails ripped them apart. Once they had fallen off in tatters, the nails tore into his skin until his lower back and thighs were one open wound. From time to time Van Cauter aimed kicks at his head, or brought his foot down heavily on the man's shoulders to stop him struggling. He also struck him with the axe handle.

Bakanja was howling with pain. "White man," he gasped, "I'll die!"

"What the (curse) do you think I care? Hit harder! If he dies, that's my business! I'm the boss in this place! I'm not having any of those Mon Père people here!"

Bongele lost count of the blows. He reckoned it must have been at least 200 - maybe 250. There was blood everywhere. The flogging went on until Bongele - despite his terror of Van Cauter - was physically unable to lift his arm any longer.

Bakanja couldn't stand up. His friends wanted to carry him, but Van Cauter shouted at them to leave him be. He was dragged by the security guards to the smoking shed, where Van Cauter fitted a set of iron fetters round his ankles. The fetters had a heavy weight attached, and the manager fastened them with a padlock. After Van Cauter had gone, Bakanja's workmates crowded into the shed. Some of the women were in tears.

Mputu asked, "Where were you going when Longange called to you on the road?"

"I was going into the bushes. And afterwards, to say my prayers. I wasn't going off anywhere."

"Why was it that Longange beat you?"

"I didn't steal anything from him! I haven't taken anything from the white man! Longange didn't want me to say my prayers."

Completely bewildered, Mputu tried to ask what "prayers" meant, but for the moment Bakanja was unable to reply. He was writhing in pain.

"Longange is a very bad white"

Back at the bungalow Ndoma, one of Giret's servants, burst out at Van Cauter, "You - killing that houseboy with a whip like that - and for no reason!"

"It wasn't for no reason," growled the manager. "Look here - in Europe when anyone steals something, even if it's only a shirt button, we cut his head off. Here, we kill him with a whip. He stole some bottles of wine off me. That's what I thrashed him for!"

Van Cauter was actually getting frightened. Why else should he be suddenly thinking up excuses? Nobody believed him. Ndoma spat out: "You're lying!" Giret quickly intervened and silenced him. Van Cauter's eyes, avoiding Ndoma's, fell on the Bongila headman. "Emeka!" he said in a gay tone of voice. "If you see any-one at Bongila who wears his baptism on his neck, hit him hard! You get me?" Emeka replied quickly that there weren't any Christians at Bongila.

Later, when Giret was alone with his own men, he told Ndoma, "Don't try to argue with that white. Longange is a wicked man - you've no idea how he'll react."

Emeka noticed that the rosary Boongo normally wore was nowhere to be seen. He asked him why he'd hidden it. Boongo replied, "So Longange won't see it, or he'll beat me like he did with Bakanja." Emeka told him not to worry; Van Cauter wasn't his boss and he didn't live at Ikili.

That evening Iyongo found Van Cauter sorting through some cards and papers he had spread out over the table. They were Bakanja's employment records, which he had brought with him and handed over to the Ikili manager as his current boss. Holding up a sheath of papers, Van Cauter told Iyongo: "This Bakanja is a slave. He doesn't belong to any village. He can't be a houseboy - he's a state employee."

As the manager knew, state enterprises depended heavily on various forms of what was effectively slave labour. If Bakanja turned out to be a runaway who'd broken his contract, it was hardly likely that anyone would wish to make a fuss about what had happened to him. Iyongo saw Van Cauter pick up another piece of paper and read it, then throw it away, muttering, "What's that for? Meddling priests!" At the time he didn't understand what the boss was talking about. Later, when he himself became a Christian, he realised it must have been Bakanja's baptism certificate.

Noticing that Iyongo was still in the room, the manager said, "We don't have any of this 'Mon Père' stuff in Europe. No one gives a (curse) for 'Mon Père' in Europe, not any more. It's past history. We've got rid of them."

Iyongo asked, "Where did you put them, to get rid of them?" Then after a pause, "What is 'Mon Père'?"

"We don't want 'Mon Père' around any more." growled the manager. They're dangerous. They tell you lies."

"But in that case, why did you let 'Mon Père' come over here?"

"They're a filthy bunch!"

Iyongo knew better than to take everything the white man said at face value. He thought to himself, "If 'Mon Père' is something from the past, and something bad, why does Bulamatari let them come here?"

Tramping back with his men to Bongila, Giret told them, "That Longange is a very bad white." Tapping his forehead he added, "He's not right in the head." Ndoma suggested that Van Cauter would be sent to prison for killing the houseboy. Wearily, Giret replied, "No, they won't put him in prison."

Bakanja lay face down in the smoking shed for three days. Even if he hadn't been chained up he could hardly have moved. Each night, after darkness fell, Mputu and Iyongo secretly brought him food.

Bakanja in hiding

Commercial Director Grillet might arrive at any moment for the inspection. However willing he was to cover up for Van Cauter, it wouldn't do to be caught with a smoking gun. On 5th February Van Cauter ordered Reynders to go back to his sub-station at Isoko to a while, telling him, "I'll send your 'boy' on after you. Grillet might come and we don't want him to see."

Van Cauter stalked over to the smoking shed and unlocked Bakanja's fetters. "Your white man is going back to Isoko. You have to go with him."

"How can I go?" gasped Bakanja. "I can't walk."

"Don't give me that. If you don't disappear right now, you'll get another whipping. You're not my 'boy'; you've got to go with your boss!"

Groaning with pain and bent almost double, Bakanja began dragging himself along the road to Isoko. As soon as he was well out of sight of Van Cauter he changed course, crawling across the estate until he reached the marsh near where it joined the path to Iyele. There he hid himself behind a tree.

Towards evening Lokwa, the estate goatherd, was rounding up the goats to shut them up for the night. As he passed near the marsh he heard a voice calling softly to him. "Lokwa," whispered Bakanja, "ask Mputu to bring me a jacket, something to make a fire with and something to eat. I'm cold."

Meanwhile Van Cauter had received a message from Reynders to say that Bakanja hadn't arrived in Isoko. It would be great if that "Mon Père" brute had collapsed on the way and died somewhere in the jungle, but it was worrying not to be sure. Suppose he was hiding somewhere near the estate? He told Iyongi, "If you see Bakanja or hear where he's hiding himself, the moment you know anything, come and tell me. Then I'll go and kill him. Understood?"

Iyongo meekly assured the manager that he'd understood perfectly. He had no idea where Bakanja was - but if he did find out, he wasn't going to breathe a word.

Van Cauter next sent word to the villagers at Ikili that if they found Bakanja they should finish him off. If only they'd do that it would be a weight off his mind. After all, Bakanja was a stranger from downriver - nothing to do with anyone round here. When he questioned Mputu and the other staff, telling them that Bakanja was missing, they opened their eyes wide and let out murmurs of great astonishment. Van Cauter couldn't work out whether to believe them or not. He snapped: "If I find him, I'll kill him!"

Despite the manager's vigilance, Mputu managed to go on sneaking food out to the marsh for the next couple of days without being caught.

An inspector arrives

Late morning on 7th February, shouts from the path alerted Van Cauter that a company steamer, the "Sanford", was approaching along the river. Hoping this would be Grillet at last, and that he could get the inspection over with, he led an excited crowd down to the landing stage at Iyele. But the visitor turned out to be Dörpinghaus. He was on his way to join Grillet in Isongu, but the steamer was in no hurry and he'd be happy to stay for lunch. Van Cauter sent Iyongo running back to Ikili to lay another place at table. As he emerged from the marsh, the lad almost fell over Bakanja. Bakanja asked him if it was Grillet who'd arrived.

"No," replied Iyongo. "It isn't Bongende, it's Potama. Anyway, how come you're not in Isoko?"

"How could I have got to Isoko? Van Cauter only sent me so I'd die on the way, and I don't want that."

Iyongo could hear the main party approaching. "Bakanja," he whispered, "Hide quickly behind that tree. Longange's coming together with Potama. When Potama comes back to the boat, show yourself to him then - but not now!"

Bakanja hid so that the white men wouldn't see him. A few minutes after they had disappeared from view Moy'a Mputsu, Dörpinghaus' headman, reached the spot. Hearing Bakanja calling to him, he asked what had happened. Bakanja said, "The white man beat me for no reason... This is the honest truth: the white man beat me because I was a Christian. He didn't want people round him who'd been baptised, and I'm a Christian. If you see my mother, if you go to the judge, if you meet the Father, tell them I'm dying because I'm a Christian."

Moy'a Mputsu tried to reassure him. "You're not going to die. You've had a lot of pain, but give it time and your wounds will heal!"

"No way! I'm going to die. I can't feel anything good any more in my body. My friend, when I was at Bompembe with my boss I saw you there. Don't be against me because I'm from downriver. Help me. Show me to your white man."

"Don't worry," replied Moy'a Mputsu. "I won't do anything against you. I'm his headman and I'll tell him about your suffering."

Van Cauter wants to kill him

After the meal the inspector and his staff set out to return to the river, followed by Lokwa who was carrying half a goat carcass given by Van Cauter as a present to Dörpinghaus. As they cleared the estate, Moy'a Mputsu began to put his employer in the picture. A little further on the inspector found Bakanja lying, face down, across the path in front of him. "White man," he said, "see how Longange's flogged me - and for no reason! I don't know what I've done wrong!"

Dörpinghaus ordered Lokwa, "Go and fetch your boss!"

Hearing from Lokwa what had happened, Van Cauter shouted for the guard who was just coming back from a hunt, carrying his gun. "Iseboyo, go and bring Bakanja here. If he won't come, kill him! I want him here!"

Seeing the guard charging towards him, still carrying his gun, Dörpinghaus stuck out his arms and blocked the path. "Go back where you came from!"

Van Cauter, approaching from behind, urged Iseboyo on: "Move, get on with it! Kill him!"

Dörpinghaus challenged Iseboyo again: "Where do you think you're going with that gun? Hunting? What are you hunting - wild pig? This is a human being!"

Van Cauter stepped round Iseboyo and went straight for Bakanja, fists flying: "Are you going to tell another white man what I did? I'm in charge round here!" Dörpinghaus pulled him off, and a furious argument began in French. Here and there the Africans caught words they recognised: "judge ... tribunal ... prison ..." Suddenly Van Cauter broke off and began shouting again at the injured man still lying on the ground. "You've lied to my boss! I'm in charge here!" So saying he plunged his fist into Bakanja's face. Dörpinghaus grabbed Van Cauter, holding his flailing arms while his staff picked Bakanja up and carried him onto the steamer. Out of his mind with rage, the manager seemed oblivious to his own blood welling up where his knuckles had hit his victim's teeth.

"It was because Bakanja was a Christian"

Getting to the truth

On the boat, Dörpinghaus bathed Bakanja's wounds and applied medication. Reaching Isongu two days later, he had him carried to the Commercial Director's house. With the evidence staring him in the face, Grillet knew he had no choice but to take action. A company steamer took him to Iyele together with another SAB agent named Stronck. Van Cauter was to pack his bags immediately. He had been relieved of his post and would not be coming back, so must take all his belongings with him, and his personal servants: to put it bluntly, he would be leaving the service of the company for the time being, in order to be available to help the police with their enquiries. The steamer departed the same day with Grillet and Van Cauter on board. Stronck was left in charge at Ikili. His first act was to carry out an inventory. It revealed that a significant quantity of rubber was unaccountably missing. Stronck also found a number of women from Bonjoli still imprisoned in the smoking shed, and set them free.

Van Cauter disembarked at Busira under the eyes of a shocked crowd of Africans. Boya, Bakanja's cousin, and several others stepped forward. "White man, why did you murder our friend?"

"It was my headman who beat him. Nothing to do with me." He strode on up the road.

Bakanja's friends asked Iyongo if it was true that the headman was allowed to do such a thing. Iyongo said innocently, "Have you ever seen a headman whip a white man's houseboy without having been told to?"

"Then ...?

"It was because Bakanja was a Christian, and Longange is a bad white!"

As soon as the household was settled into its new quarters, Iyongo and Mputu's wife went to see one of the Catholic catechists, Joseph Bakombo, and enrolled for instruction. Bakombo gave them holy medals to wear with an engraving of St Benedict on the front. When Van Cauter saw Iyongo's he shouted, "What's that? Don't say you're wearing that paraphernalia now? Get rid of it!"

Iyongo replied "No, I won't! Everyone's wearing them!"

Van Cauter's face fell. He muttered that the servants had all gone round the twist. He raved on for some time about cutting off their heads, slitting their throats. None of them took any notice.

Enquiries were instituted about the missing rubber at Ikili. Van Cauter composed a letter, stating that on several occasions he had seen parties of thieves with torches, stealing rubber from the stores, and that he'd gone after them but never caught anyone. Such a story, uncorroborated and only emerging after the deficit was discovered, the company found impossible to believe. Van Cauter was made to reimburse the value of the missing rubber to the SAB.

Boya went to Inspector Grillet to ask for permission to go to Isongu to bring back his cousin and look after him. Grillet told him it was all nonsense: this story about Bakanja being beaten was a load of rubbish. Boya was sure Grillet was lying to him, but dared not attempt the journey without a pass.

A perfunctory investigation

Rumours about what had happened were flying thick and fast throughout the region. Ifaso, a fellow-villager of Bakanja who worked on an SAB steamer, laid a formal complaint with the tribunal in Coquilhatville. Someone - possibly Ifaso himself - helpfully handed over a whip with nails in, claimed to be the "murder weapon". Vocht, the Procurator, knew he was obliged to institute an enquiry. He travelled on an SAB steamer, the "President Urban", to Iyele but didn't bother to go up to the rubber plantation. Instead he summoned a few witnesses to meet him on the boat.

When Reynders arrived he asked him, "Is it true Van Cauter killed your houseboy?" Reynders said no; Bakanja wasn't dead. The Procurator then displayed the whip and asked if it was the one Van Cauter had used on Bakanja.

Reynders replied that it wasn't; Van Cauter had taken the whip with him, packed in his trunk. Vocht was relieved to be able to complete his report, noting that whatever the truth of the matter, the statements made in Coquilhatville were grossly exaggerated. When, a short while later, Stronck arrived at the landing stage to give his evidence, the steamer had already left.

Intense sufferings and prayer

In Isongu the Head Surveyor, Dufourd, had been made responsible for ensuring that Bakanja was properly cared for while he recovered from his injuries. Dufourd summoned the local village chief, Isangankoi, and arranged for Bakanja to stay in the chief's house. He was there for four months. Two young boys were told off to keep watch over him, bathe his wounds and cook his meals using food supplied daily by the SAB. As he lay helpless on his bed, they noticed how he spent much of the time praying. It was something they couldn't make sense of, since they knew nothing about Christianity. Only later, when catechists arrived in the village, did they make the connection: "When they pray, it's like what Bakanja used to do."

On 6th April Bakanja was given a thorough examination by a police officer, who subsequently made an official deposition stating that the young man was unable to walk without assistance and, in spite of the careful nursing he had been given since being brought to

Isongu, was clearly still in a lot of pain and would be for weeks to come.

On 1st June Dufourd took Bakanja on board the "Brughman" down the river. The steamer arrived at Busira on 4th June, and Bakanja was handed over to his cousin. Since Boya wasn't in a position to care properly for an invalid himself, he lodged him with a family in an outlying village.

One day Antoine Loleka, the head catechist, came to have a word with Boya. He thought it wasn't a good idea to leave Bakanja in that village, which was too far out for them to get to quickly if anything happened. If Bakanja was going to die, he should die among his friends and relations, and fellow-Christians. Boya agreed. They found new lodgings for Bakanja with a woman named Bolangi, a wife in a polygamous marriage, who had her own house just opposite Loleka's in the African settlement of Wenga just outside Busira. Day and night he lay there on a bed, face down because his wounds still made it impossible to turn onto his back. His meals were brought to him by Boya or Loleka. A married woman named Marie Saola, who was a Christian, also helped care for him.

"I'll pray for him in heaven!"

Fr Kaptein was touring the Busira district, accompanied by Fr Georges Dubrulle. Wherever they went they noticed that people were showing unusual interest in their message. They arrived in Busira on 24th July, and Loleka took them across to see Bakanja. Fr Kaptein heard his confession and administered the Anointing of the Sick. Next morning Fr Dubrulle gave him Holy Communion. The Trappist Superior returned directly from Busira to Coquilhatville on an SAB steamer, while Fr Dubrulle stayed on for a few days. During these days he made regular visits to Bakanja, accompanied by Loleka.

"Isidore," began the priest. "Why did the white man beat you?"

"The white man didn't like Christians! He didn't want me to wear the 'habit of Mary'. He told me off if I said my prayers."

Although Boya had obtained more medication from Grillet, Bakanja's wounds showed no sign of healing. They were now badly infected and giving him terrible pain, and his hip-bone could be seen sticking out. Fr Dubrulle tried to comfort him. He said simply, "It doesn't matter if I die. If God wants me to live, I'll live. If God wants me to die, I'll die. It's all the same to me."

Forgiveness

Fr Dubrulle tried to remind Bakanja of the importance of forgiveness. He mustn't die nursing hatred in his heart against Van Cauter. He replied: "I'm not angry with the white man. If he beat me that's his problem, not mine. If I die, I'll pray for him in heaven!"

On his return to Bamania, Fr Dubrulle couldn't stop talking about how deeply touched he had been by Bakanja's courage and patience, his spirit of forgiveness.

Last moments and death

Up to this point Bakanja had remained lucid. But during the next few weeks he spoke less and less, and when he did it was often difficult to understand him. He was clearly in atrocious pain. The smell of gangrene from the infected tissues around his wounds was getting worse, and Bolangi began complaining; was this going to go on for ever? Loleka then took the invalid into his own house, setting aside a space for him on the verandah.

On Sunday 15th August 1909 Bakanja suddenly began spitting blood. After bringing up a lot of blood and putrid matter, he clearly felt better. He got up and, still holding his rosary, went to walk in a grove of banana trees that stood alongside Loleka's house. Everyone was amazed - it was so long since he'd been able to stand, or even sit upright. After a little while he went back to his bed and lay down.

Later that morning the Catholics gathered at Loleka's house for Morning Prayer. Afterwards Bakanja said to Marie Saola, "Marie, I'd like to eat some surelle." Surelle is a tropical fruit that is usually eaten cooked; it's not nice raw. Marie willingly went off and cooked some for him, and he ate it. Delighted to see him showing such a good appetite, she went off home to cook him some more. As she returned carrying the dish, someone came to tell her that Bakanja had just that moment given up his soul to God.

His friends made a rough stretcher and carried his body to the cemetery, where they buried him with his rosary still clutched in his hand as it had been at the moment of his death.

Van Cauter in the dock

During 1909 Van Cauter returned on leave to Belgium, sailing in the same ship as the Grillets. Stronck, also home on leave, met him in Brussels, and they went into a café to have a drink together. Van Cauter was in fine form, boasting about his exploits in the Congo - the hostage-taking, reprisals against villages, the constant need for brutality to keep the natives in line, and so on. He still had the chicotte with the nails - he'd kept it as a souvenir - and he proudly showed Stronck the little scar on his finger where he'd punched Bakanja in Dörpinghaus' presence. Stronck warned him to keep his voice down.

In January 1910 a tribunal in Coquilhatville found Van Cauter guilty of abusing his authority over the black personnel of the Ikili estate, by causing the infliction on Bakanja of blows resulting in incapacity to work. Remarking that "The consideration that the motive of the accused was to violate Bakanja's personal ethical code, and the principle of religious freedom, makes his act all the more odious." the judge sentenced him to two-and-a-half years' penal servitude and a fine of 500 francs. He could not be tried for murder because, although it was generally known that Bakanja had died from his injuries, no legal proof could be produced. The verdict was given in absentia, because the culprit had skipped bail. He was rumoured to be somewhere up in the north of the colony, back in his old trade of gun-running and ivory smuggling.

By August 1912 Van Cauter had been apprehended and was being held on remand in Coquilhatville while his case went to appeal. Having had plenty of time to elaborate his story, he insisted that he'd ordered Bakanja given a mere 17 lashes, for stealing from him and from Reynders, and also because the "boy" was a dangerous incendiary who had been caught inciting the estate workers to desert. As for the whip, it was true he'd had to mend it and had used a bit of wire for the purpose. Afterwards, Bakanja had treated himself with native medicines to make the wounds look worse than they really were; he'd done this out of spite, to get his boss into trouble. However this version of events was contradicted by the clear and detailed eye-witness testimony given at the original hearing by Reynders and Grillet, Iyongo, Bongele and Bomandjoli. The judgment against Van Cauter was confirmed.

The absolute impunity previously enjoyed by SAB agents in Bus-Bloc had been severely dented: from 1909 to 1913 increasing numbers of agents were tried before the Coquilhatville tribunal on charges of physical cruelty, and 34 were found guilty.

"They pray the same way Bakanja prayed"

Although Van Cauter had alleged that Bakanja was continually trying to convert the other staff, this claim is not backed up by their own testimony. In any case he seems to have complied promptly with Van Cauter's prohibition against praying with them. Nevertheless he had proved an astonishingly effective evangelist - not through words, but through the calm simplicity of his life, and the faithfulness which had led to his death. In all the places where his presence had briefly touched people's lives, hundreds and thousands were now flocking into the Church.

In September 1913, at a meeting of the ecclesiastical superiors in the Congo, it was resolved that a thorough investigation be made into the facts of the "Bakanja affair", with a view either to introducing a cause in Rome for his beatification, or "at least to provide preachers with an example which it would be most fruitful to refer to". Mgr Van Ronsle communicated the resolution to the Trappists and asked them to arrange for an enquiry.

Although there could still be no priests' residence in Busira itself, there was now a permanent mission station at Bokote a little way upriver. Bus-Bloc had been served since 1910 by an enthusiastic young itinerating missionary, Fr Aloysius Dewitte, and already had 13 chapels with a resident catechist, and 4,000 baptised Christians. Dewitte had noticed how often, when catechists first arrived in a new village, people remarked: "They pray the same way Bakanja prayed." Over a period of six months, as he travelled around fulfilling his pastoral duties, he tracked down eyewitnesses of the key events in Bakanja's life and interviewed them.

Iyongo had been baptised and Mputu was receiving instruction. Even so, both of them were very frightened and reluctant to tell all they knew; Fr Dewitte had to interview them several times before he got their full stories. He had been asked particularly to establish whether there was any truth in Van Cauter's allegation that Bakanja was a thief. The witnesses insisted unanimously that there was no truth whatsoever. Iyongo explained that he himself had the keys to Van Cauter's stores, and nobody could have taken anything without his knowledge.

Iseboyo, who had committed a murder while in Van Cauter's service, was on the run from the police. He had joined a band of outlaws living deep in the jungle, nearly a day's march from Bongila. His brother agreed to take the priest to him, but the outlaws suspected a trick and threatened to shoot the visitors full of arrows. Dewitte and his party turned back, but Iseboyo followed secretly behind and eventually hailed them from a safe distance, standing at a spot where Dewitte couldn't actually see him. He agreed to answer questions from where he was, so long as no one tried to approach him.

At the little cemetery used by the Christians of Busira, Marie Saola pointed out the spot where Bakanja lay buried.

Altogether Dewitte obtained the testimonies of 24 people - mostly Africans, though Stronck, and another SAB agent not directly involved in the incident, also agreed to testify. Unlike the tribunal, Dewitte could not oblige anyone to give evidence, and presumably Reynders, if still in Bus-Bloc, would have refused. Dörpinghaus had resigned from the SAB, and gone home to write a book in which he described what he had witnessed in the Congo, and appealed to the German government to press Belgium for effective action.

Cover-up

News from the Trappist mission in the Congo was circulated to supporters in Flanders through a little magazine called Het Missiewerk, edited and produced at Westmalle. The concerns of the missionaries about the abusive treatment of Africans, which they so often had to witness, and the harassment in religious matters meted out both to them and to their converts, were presumably reported in confidential correspondence, but no word of these problems was ever allowed to appear in Het Missiewerk. Nevertheless the story of the conflict between the Trappists and the SAB was picked up by

Belgian newspapers, to the acute embarrassment of the
company and the Colonial Ministry. The government
responded by assuring the missionaries of its good inten-
tions, and promising to resolve the difficulties if only they
would co-operate and stop stirring up trouble. The missionaries had, of course, heard such promises before.
Even so, could they afford to alienate the government,
whose support for the Catholic missions would be discon-
tinued unless they fell into line?

Both sides appealed to Rome. The Papal Nuncio and
the Bishop of Namur intervened, urging the Vatican
Secretary of State, Raphael Cardinal Merry del Val, to
conciliate the government by imposing silence on the
missionaries about everything that had happened in the
Congo up to that date. After two earlier drafts had been
rejected by the government, as putting too much empha-
sis on the reasons behind the dispute, the final version of
the fateful letter was signed by the Cardinal on 31st
December 1913. When therefore, in April 1914, Dewitte
presented the results of his Enquiry, his superiors already
knew it could not be made public.

During the night of 28th May 1917, with the assistance
of two African volunteers, Fr Dewitte secretly exhumed
the remains of Isidore Bakanja, keeping a careful record
of the details. He hid them for a week in the chapel at
Busira, and in early June took them to Bokote. There he
placed the bones in a specially-made redwood casket, and

reburied them in the churchyard. Bakanja's scapular and rosary, which had been found in the grave, were placed in a separate box. The tomb was marked by strewing over it several layers of pulverised brick.

Crisis in the Trappist Mission

Dewitte's undisguised disapproval of the cruelty and religious harassment suffered by the Africans at the hands of the company agents was upsetting the SAB. The matter came to a head when he publicly advised a group of workers to look for jobs elsewhere; the reforms introduced into the colonial system by the Belgian government allowed them to do this, and a significant number acted on the advice. At the SAB's insistence, Fr Kaptein removed Dewitte from Bokote. He tried hard to come to terms with his superior's decision, but his sense of bitterness and discouragement overwhelmed him, and in 1923 he walked out. As a priest and professed religious he was not free to marry in the eyes of the Church, but he formed a stable relationship with an African woman and had two children with her, supporting himself and his family as a businessman. A copy of his Enquiry was sent to Westmalle with other papers relating to his case, and locked up in the confidential section of the archives.

His departure from the Order had taken place against a background of disruption and uncertainty as Westmalle resolved to abandon the Congo mission, judging it unsuited to the Trappist charism. The Sacred Heart Missionaries took it over in 1924. The previous incumbents naturally had to remain in post for a while to teach the newcomers the language, and ensure a smooth transition. In the event fifteen of them - including Fr Dubrulle - transferred to the Sacred Heart congregation in order to stay on. The remaining monks returned to Belgium.

Dewitte brought up his children in the Catholic faith, and remained on good terms with his former confrères, often helping them out in practical ways. They felt considerable sympathy for him, and eventually, in 1952, managed to obtain permission from Rome for his position to be regularised, so that he could return to the sacraments. During his last illness he was repatriated to Belgium for treatment, and died in Brussels in a hospital run by the Little Sisters of the Poor.

He had never forgotten the story of Bakanja. His son, Camille Mboko, later recalled "What my Dad said to me was this: 'Bakanja was flogged, but what made him a real saint was the greatness of the prayer, the Our Father.' Because when they took him to Wenga to the catechist Loleka's house, the Father asked him: "Isidore, now you are near to death, what are you going to do about those who killed you?" Bakanja answered him: "We often pray the Our Father, saying: Forgive us our trespasses, as we forgive those who have trespassed against us. Before God forgives us, it's right that we forgive our brothers first.""

After my Dad said that, he burst into tears. And that is the most important thing he told me."

A copy of the Enquiry remained in a drawer at Bokote. Also, Fr Dubrulle had composed a brief narrative account of the life and death of Isidore Bakanja, with a view to publication. Though never published, it was available to be read by the Sacred Heart Missionaries, and many of them certainly knew the story of Bakanja. However they rarely spoke of it. Any priest who showed interest in it, and noticed that it was still vividly remembered by the African Christians, was advised to drop the matter so not to upset the SAB. The official line was clear: the story must not be publicised because:

- it would show the whites in a bad light; and
- the missionary who conducted the Enquiry had left the priesthood.

A cross had been erected by the piptadenia africana tree at the edge of the marsh near Ikili, behind which Bakanja had hidden. People used to meet to say the rosary there. As the years passed, the details of the story were almost forgotten, but people still knelt and made the sign of the cross when passing the spot. For many years the tomb in Bokote was carefully tended, and prayers were said there. But during the chaotic period when the Congo gained its independence in 1960, a flood wrecked the churchyard and obliterated the grave markers, and most people forgot all about it.

Independence

Within a few years General Mobutu established a military dictatorship. Wanting to mark a clean break with the old days of colonial oppression, he changed the name of the country to Zaire. (His successor would eventually change it back.) Cosmetic measures Mobutu could manage. What he could not do was bring his country either peace or prosperity.

Suggestions in Church circles that now, surely, was the time to bring "the Bakanja affair" back into the light of day went on being dismissed as inopportune. Despite the continued misgivings, in 1975 a search was made in the Westmalle archives for Dewitte's Enquiry, and it was sent to Mgr Frédéric Etsou, who was then Bishop of Mbandaka (the new name for Coquilhatville). Copies were also sent to all the other Congolese Bishops. In August 1976 the Mbandaka diocesan catechists held a meeting in which they presented an official request to the Bishop to proceed with the cause for beatification.

A diocesan enquiry was launched. Teachers and cate-chists began once again to know and tell the story of Isidore Bakanja, and in May 1980, during a visit to Kisangani, Pope John Paul II spoke warmly of his exam-ple. In February 1985 an old man named Ikelya indicated the forgotten site of Bakanja's tomb in the churchyard at Bokote, next to a termite nest. The relics were enclosed in an ebony chest close to the baptismal font in the church.

In 1987 the findings of the diocesan enquiry were presented to Rome. Since Bakanja had suffered martyrdom
for his faithfulness to the devotion of the scapular, the
Carmelite Postulator, Fr Redemptus Valabek, happily took
on the case. Sacred Heart Missionary Fr Honoré Vinck
agreed to serve as *Promotor Fidei*, and Westmalle Abbey
offered a contribution towards the financial expenses.

Beatification

The ceremony of beatification of Isidore Bakanja at last
took place in Rome on 24th April 1994, during the
Special Assembly for Africa of the Synod of Bishops. In
his homily Pope John Paul II declared:

"You were a man of heroic faith, Isidore Bakanja,
young layman of Zaire. As a baptised person, called to
spread the Good News, you shared your faith and witness
to Christ with such conviction that to your companions you
seemed one of those valiant lay faithful, the catechists.
Yes, Blessed Isidore, absolutely faithful to your baptismal
promises, you were a true catechist, toiling generously for
'the Church in Africa and for her evangelising mission'...

Isidore, your sharing in the paschal mystery of Christ, in
the supreme work of his love, was total. Because you
desired to be loyal to your baptismal faith whatever the cost,
you suffered scourging like your Master. Like your Master
on the Cross, you forgave your persecutors; and you showed
yourself to be a builder of peace and reconciliation."

CTS
MEMBERSHIP

We hope you have enjoyed reading this booklet. If you would like to read more of our booklets or find out more about CTS - why not do one of the following?

1. Join our Readers CLUB.
We will send you a copy of every new booklet we publish, - through the post to your address. You'll get 20% off the price too.

2. Support our work and Mission.
Become a CTS Member. Every penny you give will help spread the faith throughout the world. What's more, you'll be entitled to special offers exclusive to CTS Members.

3. Ask for our Information Pack.
Become part of the CTS Parish Network by selling CTS publications in your own parish.

Call us now on 020 7640 0042 or return this form to us at CTS, 40-46 Harleyford Road, London SE11 5AY
Fax: 020 7640 0046 email: info@cts-online.org.uk

❏ I would like to join the *CTS Readers Club*

❏ Please send me details of how to join CTS as a *Member*

❏ Please send me a *CTS Information Pack*

Name:..

Address:..

....

Post Code:...

Phone: ....

email address: ....

Registered charity no. 218951.
Registered in England as a company limited by guarantee no.57374.